The Beholder

Kate Behrens was born in 1959, one of twin daughters to two painters. A runner up in the 2010 Mslexia poetry competition, she lives in Oxfordshire, and has one daughter.

The Beholder

Kate Behrens

TWO
RIVERS
PRESS

821.92

First published in the UK in 2012 by Two Rivers Press
7 Denmark Road, Reading RG1 5PA.
www.tworiverspress.com

ISBN 978-1-901677-83-6

British Library Cataloguing in Publication Data. A catalogue record
for this book is available from the British Library.

1 2 3 4 5 6 7 8 9

Two Rivers Press is represented in the UK by Inpress Ltd and
distributed by Central Books.

Cover design by Nadja Guggi using Pete Hay's illustrations
Text design by Nadja Guggi and typeset in Janson and Parisine.
Frontispiece © Kate Behrens 2012. Untitled etching by the author.

Printed and bound in Great Britain by Imprint Digital, Exeter.

To Celeste

Acknowledgements

Without Elke Asmus, *The Beholder* would not exist.
My daughter, Celeste Harber and Simon Frazer both
contributed to its making with patient help and moral
support, Peter Robinson through his generosity of spirit
as editor and publisher and John Froy, also of the Two
Rivers Press, for kindly initiating the process. Deepest
thanks to them all.

Thanks to my family for their loyalty – to Soph for the
daring of her own lines.

The title poem, 'The Beholder', first appeared in *Portfolio:
Dartington Hall School Artists 1926-1987* ed. Alice Leach
(Brightsea Press, 2011).

Contents

Mixing our Metaphors

After three days
the room was as iridescent
as inside a soap balloon.
Instead of a screaming baby
I got the spirit of Christmas
inside a planet
as tightly closed as a walnut –
then expanses of virgin snow.
It was the hottest day of July.
We lay in the sliced shreds
of my long pink t-shirt
on the sweat-soaked sheet
mixing our metaphors.
I who had also
just been born
would hold up the sky for you.

Washing-line in Segovia

A washing-line of blue notes
excavated from blue ground
in blue and steepening dusk

in counterpoint of starlings and SEATs
away from the stained fingering sun
busy in homes of pipistrelle
high up in the aqueduct

left a stranger weird or desired
from their own desiring
as if they were both inside an experiment
altered through surveillance

or out-of-scale big greys of leaves
suggesting they could knit themselves
over the bandstand assembling
into a foreign blood stream.

Blue note – a flattened note characteristic of the blues.
Blue ground – a conglomerate in which diamonds are found.

Henge

If they chipped at the blocks
as horizons, they cared not
for the monument
since the Ancestors made the hills,
built stars to shine in
the purposeful curves
of water weaving through land
and there was no landscape but for themselves
moving through nuances
of sound and light
till granite came slowly down
to meet with their bodies' notations.

Memorial Party

As the canapés to and fro
and the champagne diminishes,
the woman in diamante
and towering heels collapses.
Then there are the speeches.
In the ensuing silence,
two hundred half-remembered fucks
invigorate the grieving faces –
eyeballs slide beneath
the hooded lids and raw-silk turbans.
The ghost is drinking somewhere else.

Invited for their piquancy
against the eau-de-nil
and for nostalgic reasons,
five black boys stand against the wall
revealing nothing but their stillness.

Thirty-Three Roars

It knew the wetness, the texture
of strata, the shocks
of small rocks falling
the speed, exact
for the hearts and bones constricted
by steel and self-possession –

aimed at the azure, shaped
like an apple corer, it
opened cage doors as if
a mystic's imagination
was expelling canaries
into a moon-landing
a field of sun-lit feathers
knees falling, dust
and ordinary things –

thirty-three roars
went up from the world
for loves in premature
graves and their timely
exhumations
or from love's lacking
or for the loves
that had always been.

Divorce

The snowman squeaks laboriously
while the green grows bigger fast
surprising your garden –
meanwhile your dad plays bagatelle
delaying your grief
pulls funny faces through the glass.

Disguised as the Air

Between the chair and table
a musculature
of negative shapes.
The apple tree thrives
on the ashes of others.
All that I give you
leaves me richer.
Only as corpses
are we entire.
If I hold back my knowing
you might find your own.
You can steal my car
but not my dance-floor.
The hole in the stone
makes for a wish.
The oyster tastes only of sea.
Thanks to what binds me
I am free for a moment.
The lopped-off branches
speed up the greening.
The sun in the monastery
slants through a void.
Love lies hidden
in what is missing.
This bird invents
from a handful of notes.

Views from a Restaurant Car

The journey, arrested there
cleaned of the floaters
mysteriously – (his boat
leaving and
leaving her)

now recalled
how the rocking sierras'
exaltation of blues

had from a great distance
fingered the little mouths
of her hips.

It was thanks to the nothing-at-all
here, but unsmellable
stretches of dark
bleeding with trickles of flaming herbs
all along the earth's rim

the something-other-than-sun
descending
to stall the imaginable animals.

In Quentin Bell's Jug

This jug was made by Quentin Bell.
The daffs were grown in chemicals
in Manchester – God's little finger
tickled the bulbs.
Already nicotine-orange,
the leaves caress the one-day flowers
turning translucent buff,
huddling against the green
of Nature Corners.
The buds are their secret weapon –
death by lime to Pheasant Eye,
supercilious Scilly Isles,
death to Bloomsbury splashes –
think ampoules,
the silk of a praying mantis,
protuberance, a sexy emerald
ribbon cinching a mantis waist.
A short raffia, biscuit skirt.
Kisses of newborn to dying.
The colours of poster paint.
There's a whole family, Quentin,
shouting through their malnutrition,
'Wa-hey! The spring is coming!'

The Beholder

Pablito, back home, says 'let me fix it' –
tangled up in the wires, his mother's face
is one small juniper
or a piece of that gravel he offered up
to the nest of an absent dog.
His father back-fires like an obstacle
for the sake of a blue remark.
Someone is slowly falling over
down on the Rua Arenas.
Pablito sees camellias now,
the dun-edged blossoms
she gathered in dreams.

Cut

An artichoke, sliced almost in half,
gleamed on the blade
the cadences of your moon-coloured
chest, bloody only with spring
under my hanging breasts
with all around us the nibs and the nodes
and re-invention of songs.

Rhomboid

At night his house
was splashed over the opposite hill
windowless, inking the oaks
between two luminous
telegraph poles, spread now
like an old tattoo
over a middle-aged back.
The frost on the brook
chugging the iced-up meat of the valley
between the hush of those shapes
made it appear like a gash
under the far away stars,
or the warmly-lit domicile
with its darker attachment
lying so deeply under his surface.

O Portiño

It was his idea
to go to O Portiño –
we had only an hour
and the sea in the cove
was sadder than tin
under a thin glass moon.
If the real thing
stood for the more romantic nouns
of 'moonlight', 'water', 'cliff',
it satisfied his Latin mind
which lacked a sense of irony
and was emboldened by
despair's libido
into a kind of hijacker of hearts.
The only weapon he owned
was passion, pure and stubborn,
now brandished at my reason
through his forming mouth
and chaotic rhythms
tapping against disappointment
half-way up my sleeve
on the homeward journey.
There was nothing more than this
except that choosing seemed a meanness
afforded by the rich receivers,
and his face convinced me.

Somebody's Lilies

This could be the layered paper
swaddling wasps
or a wood in Norway
or a house of cards

you pass a plump partridge
on a white plate

somebody's lilies
are extruding a hormone
under night's tank

I'm forking the meat through her phantom hair

The O and the Minus

At birth your irises lost their moorings.
Your mouth was an O and mine was a minus.
You were a wriggler and I was resigned.
Our soup congealed then chilled,
became the expansive sofa skin
stretched out between our spines.
We missed our clashing bones.
Egg-eyed, we stared at each other.
The moon, badly disguised as a half,
poked out a hand through the blanket
draping the curtain pole.

Making Blue Sparks

The four corners mapped it out:

a woman's stick figure
shade of black nylon

the glass with its concrete
and clay hand

my dead mother's
tapestry picture

myself in the bed
making blue sparks.

Later the picture
tousled my fingers
with her and the candles
of ancient nights.

Dad Steals a Christmas Tree

It was after the gold, the black filigree
of the journey; pre-Christmas sky
arcing aquamarine, tight over the chestnuts,
the intimate smoke threading crystal –

the mountain was over-relaxed
under its bunches of fists,
wolf-ridden and drenched,
slopping its skirts in indefinite mists.

You stopped on the hair-pin, got out –
we watched for carabinieri,
watched the edge of the verge

and just before the corpse in the flash-back
up you popped like a monkey
dragging a six foot tree.
The bungee cord snapped over the roof rack.

When the landscape gathered speed
behind the breath-dripped glass
sleep was enthralled by the edge of the blade,
the smell of Nazionali

and doors onto a safer world
hinged with roping of silver tinsel
and smelling of that elixir
drunk by Father Christmas *et al*
to make their lives eternal.

PTSD

Dirty yet holy it seemed
before the doctors gave it a name
that ritualistic sucking at screens –
always the violin concerto
and the altar of window before
kneeling towards the hills' thick tucks
the wedges of solid mist.
Over-aroused
by the rasping of now against then
it was never discussed;
one of us standing, holding
perhaps a biro or glass
whilst the other sunk into her raucous finale
rubbing the grief till it burst
too much detail over the trees.

Closed Shutters

I remembered the ears
of a flame and silver Easter egg
behind extravagant glass,
the light passing through something opaque;
also a glimpse of the duomo
through a darkened alley
not understanding what I was seeing.
I was watching bands of sunlight
over the damask cover
disappearing when angels or pigeons
passed behind closed shutters.
Dad was out buying cigarettes
and Mum had long been in Heaven.
When I opened the window
a deep bell was tolling
in the eggshell sky –
up from the street
came the scents of washed pavement,
espresso and vanilla,
the revving engines of motorini.
Hilarious shouts trailed bellies of grief.
Inside the room Dad's sweat
and washing powder like honeysuckle
mixed with the smells of plaster and stone,
the ashtray overflowing.
I folded my clothes,
carefully pressing the creases
with twelve-year-old fingers.

Taking my Leave

if you flinched
at the very first notes, whatever's dredged up
will always be secret
and the heron, pecking at tussocks
down in the ink-washed field
will stalk forwards
thoughtless beyond you

Not Flying Away

It can only be letters now –
I write to the place where
high above the Calle Huertas
you sleep among splashes and bottles.
There are over-sized sea gulls
instead of flowers
lined up on the balcony,
starched shapes on skins of blue glass
which turn yellow at dusk.
I wish you could really
see the birds, how they
are almost of this world
which you part inhabit
without the sweetness
of sea-inveigled eye,
plumage, re-balance of weight involved
in not flying, not
flying away
at the first appearance of light.

To the Edge (After Your Illness)

I cut open the parcel,
watched you sliding your shards
across the hardness of chair
like the carcass of a little boat –

I watched you open the book,
the death-lit ocean of your eye
seeming to look through its rims
at a Romanesque cupola.

I was willing you into the rings of stone,
that helmet for the disabled,
up to the blow-hole pointed at Heaven,
right to the piercing's edge

whilst the ants crawled over your fingers.
You'd dragged yourself through a blizzard of roses,
emerged with your focus swinging
over half-remembered cloisters,

the carvings by Gislebertus
at Chartres and Autun,
but your eye became as opaque as roses
floating over the ocean's surface

above that tiny circle of blue
looking back at you.

Fairytale (My Stepmother)

We passed the eucalyptus
some kind of white mimosa
through their conjoined scents
over the coastline tarmac –
you, in unlikely trainers
talking sprint techniques
and dying for a roll-up
as I was in the verges
with the stamped-out stars
of resinous seed cases
buried in the ramsons –
if he was the 'elephant'
in absentia now
we took no notice and
the cream camellia
which half blocked out the sea
had you like a Japanese
stooping over fallen blooms –
they'd need some dark green leaves
you said
to float beside them in the bowl.

Double Exposure

Under this little girl's footfall
the pavement, through it not being water,
makes day-to-day a quiet
achievement. It must be
decodeable, in flap/gape
of sole on sole, something too green
in her pelvis's stringing
into in-turned knees.

But if it is you I am following
I find only the first lurch
of transmittable earth;
a woman's un-
forgivable arms.

Now the little girl's turning the corner
the double-exposure's troubled
by straps,
bronze sandals come into focus
returning her to a singleton,
you to the edges of my awareness.

Rehearsal

Up there on the rock-shelf,
hung between ages
of un-belonging,
skin strung over
the poles of your body

the orange hillside holds you –

then sudden grace
flames
flames down through the gorge

to where the adders are swimming.

Thousands of drops
rise from the sky-blue
corona, gather

fall as roped worlds you knew.

The careless sun grins on.

To John

When John was little
life smashed him and smashed him.
He was crushed into a glitter.
Then he was told that despair was a sin.
One day in midsummer,
he lowered that bulk
sculpted by anti-psychotics
into the shape of a small gorilla,
over the edge of the precipice
like a polar bear takes to the ocean
when the ice floes are melting.
He swam towards the horizon
and the kisses of Saint Theresa.

Elephant Day

It is you who remembers to tell me,
who insists I look
at the sky more than usual –
I who takes time
to register this
is just how it was or
the very reverse.

I set about
pulling at you,
try to lay
bits of you back in the darkness,
an elephant picking at bones –

but nothing much
sticks out, only
your calloused fore-finger,
scent crumpled
up on a note
rescued from out of your bin

that day when the plane tree
dappling your desk,
a moth flapping, sunk traces
into the ice
as significant things
or witnesses –

you won't twist into the holes, back,
never did,
alive more than ever
with your head-weight of leaden smiles
and your bullets of sweetness

inside of my dreams any other
day of the year
but this.

Wren

Passing this corner
where the walls have
dragged on the seasons
and there, the flint of its pillow
above the dull foils
of the leaves, I
remember the susurration
a tiny
bird-foot stagger –
how it leant the bell
of its cheek on my house.
Its eyes were already
slits, the ferned threads
of its quills
shrugging the colours
of forest floors
its beak twisted up
as if a dream
had slid its lens
between this moment and death.
When it tumbled, its claws
became posies of wire –
its passage
from egg to head resting
five seconds here
had ended. The snow fell
from miles to its breast.

The Thrush

this idiot-savant's opening bars
stumble like drunks before
cracking its darkened audience

or a whale burning the oceans' tubes
hears a songstress, scales down
to match her tiny fibrillations

or two dimensional, it clacks
an armature, some cartilage
against the voile of five a.m.

Winter Birds

I'm chipping your shit
off the table, pouring
the steaming water –
the tireless brain
of a different longing
observes a human securing
an hour, gently unlocks
the chains of the night
lets them fall
into the leaves.
Out of the arsenic breath
their light inches
blot the seeds
before their flight's betrayed –
unable to feel
other than joy or
plummeting solid out of the trees
their unimaginably
simple clinging
to twig on the ice-burnt horizon
is held in the outline
from beak to tail
via the curve of the wings.

Yew

Here, where the yew roots' deep clench
on clutter of chalk and flint
unfolds, the melancholy arms
clothed in shredded bronze
give up their weight to the earth.
Behind the black water-
shoots, the barred horizon loses
all substance and only
this ancient thrusting being
is still; the path beyond it
frothing with light, tricks us away
with its mission
from the under-foot pulses
those held tight in the sky
the visible conduit creeping between them.

Roe Deer

Just for a second, in stillness
she tells me she could be won – her sinews
are oblivious
beginning to flush with the chemicals

to pattern her thus; sideways on
to the picket fence, legs spooled up, flying –
re-aligning into the pen
to face full-on its clanging copse.

Her head must breathe the field beyond
her knees in the grains of human smells
arrive pre-bent, optimistic
leap again without preamble.

Badger at Stonor

Then, when a shaved loop in a field
only just visible
is implying some hidden meaning,
a small bulk bowls out of the dusk,
stops short on the chalky track –
two little black moons,
tumbled out of preoccupations,
shoot up at my knees,
juggle in space for a second
as stumbling into unmoved bushes
he vanishes with improbable ease.

Spider Silk

1

You should understand
that coming at it from a
lower point
in bright colourless light
without expectation
the silk was as jewelled
as a blonde girl's hair
caught off guard
but more so –
ruby and sapphire
diamond
flashed on the track
to the barbed wire.
The hill looked askance at
the milking shed roof.
The cows travelled slowly through it.

2

So much of it on the chalk-white path

tangling the mornings' inches.
He'd sit with the toys of the landscape
come out of a trunk, cut-outs

then blood through the pasted larches
dripping blue shadows of paint.

He got old there on the bench
beyond his master's roof.

Sap

A way to burn up the hours,
the garden's spring-clean
in an Easterly wind –
the unnatural peace
is a thin sheet of glass

but the sap between embers and smoke
drips the rose which spelt out words on the window
the nest of the bird which once sang in her ribs
the nettles whose flowers
made her witnessed eyes swell –
the oils of Christmas
vertiginous springs
poking lime through the black –

her stomach no longer twitches
at robins picking up worms
nor carries the heavy burdens of storms

though her fingers still cross from their habit for cliffs –
undignified strangers
ringed by all their old fevers.

Yellow on Black

When laying her head down at last
the unwritten words crawled out of the page
and into the melting boundaries
a plane tree witnessed the ordinary window
blazing an oblong of yellow on black –
behind it Orfeo, the drooping tulips
nothing disintegrating yet.
What colour was the cover
beneath her? In the morning her desk
still clung to the floor.
Her door still opened and shut on its hinges.
A moth took over, like in a cartoon
the elongation of seconds –
fidgeted a skull to the tree.
Later the eyes of the sky snapped shut.

The Long Lens

I, at the wrong end, will stay very small
as, crossing the rain-swollen rivers
you inflate like a boat; the face which I stole
to swing through the months to September

(full for some reason, with un-swallowed water)
is free of those unsuitable boots
the open-lipped bag spilling out treasures
as, little by little, your teaching's unhooked

all the bad stars I scattered. If in that face
your very first oak's still tracing its branches
I concede its opacity, as mine must be opaque
the Bambara's shadowed in powders of shells.

The Bambara are an ethnic group from Mali,
some of whom wear a cloth dyed in fermented mud.

Night Ceiling Gels

– they were like our long-ago herds
movement's or breath's obbligato
entering into sleeplessness
to leaps of hearts unbounded from day –

stains attached to shush through rain,
(remembered words to the East
marking the start of a love-affair once,
'George Davis is innocent'
ballooning on sooty yellow bridges);
or stopped where your conscience once faltered
to black clunks muffled in night,
unsteady girls disgorged
into the realms of waiting men –

over the furrows we'd gauged out,
under a sky held in abeyance,
near to half-forgotten parks,
the skeleton leaves and harmless litter …

stains attached to shush through rain
of taxis, Ford Cortinas
missions rushed across the ceiling
to splash our eyelids closed.

Remaking Your Bed

In this boat I've trammelled your sheets –
they lie quiet, squeaking an ancient
song. And although
my grandmother's knuckles appeared
from nowhere, making hospital
corners, it wasn't really her hands
but some Latinos laying tiles
into a pattern thriving
on absence. I want it all
to be blown open
even if by continents clashing
in private colours and noises, in pain
I, unable to do anything
lie awake in scentless darkness.
This boat will be wrecked by grace.

Rehearsal at the Monastery of Comillas

After the chill of Comillas
the car, afloat with recent pictures
arrived at a man on a moon-lit bend
tying a cow to a ring on his house

my father, whose throat
still choked on a net
of dredging notes, slumped,
stub of Ducados a glow at midnight –

at one, a grand mal on the windscreen
ambiguous lights keeping the shoreline
hammered, 'alive in the city' –
he mumbled, 'scratch an atheist
and find a believing man'
as red changed to green in the suburbs.

Lights from the Night Train

Precise as to prickly lettuce
burdock and golden rod
how they slurred through transparent bodies
into the slick of elders
to re-emerge as gelder-rose
knapweed, michaelmas daisies
the compartment itself was vague
with limbs simply truncated by boulders
and light, a swift bash into its clique.

Most real, the middle ground –
lone horse stooped over sleep
poisonous tussock, stadium-lit, or
through clear and lemon glass
skimming the forgetting girders
smaller flashes of neon mouths –
even a tiny mountain
almost consumed by its own darkness.

The horse has swallowed
the very last field – grease
somehow cut,
orange inhabitant
neither the light nor the day
but emblematic, as white
sugar to snow or
stars, or the embers of flight –

and this, for now, pierceable still –
the brain of a horse
too deep in the night of its muscle
or night-train traveller
not yet so asleep

that all of these rooms might gather together
into a view.

Two Rivers Press has been publishing in and about Reading since 1994. Founded by the artist Peter Hay (1951–2003), the press continues to delight readers, local and further afield, with its varied list of individually designed, thought-provoking books.